W9-CZL-221

MONSTERS OF THE ANIMAL KINGDOM

RATS

Rachel Lynette

PowerKiDS press
New York

For Lucy, who dearly loved her rats

Published in 2013 by The Rosen Publishing Group, Inc.
29 East 21st Street, New York, NY 10010

First Edition

Editor: Jennifer Way
Book Design: Greg Tucker

Photo Credits: Cover Heiko Kiera/Shutterstock.com; p. 4 S. Cooper Digital/Shutterstock.com; pp. 5, 14 Maslov Dmitry/Shutterstock.com; p. 6 Martin Fowler/Shutterstock.com; p. 7 anatolypareev/Shutterstock.com; pp. 8–9 Geoff du Feu/Photodisc/Getty Images; p. 10 Arathrael Photography/Flickr/Getty Images; p. 11 Peter A. Kemmer/Flickr/ Getty Images; p. 11 Nature Picture Library/Britain On View/Getty Images; pp. 12–13 Paul Broadbent/Shutterstock. com; p. 15 John Downer/Taxi/Getty Images; p. 16 Gisela Delpho/Picture Press/Getty Images; p. 17 Vincent J. Musi/ National Geographic/Getty Images; p. 18 Eric Isselée/Shutterstock.com; p. 19 E. A. Janes/age fotostock/Getty Images; p. 20 Eric Gevaert/Shutterstock.com; p. 21 Four Oaks/Shutterstock.com; p. 22 Foto Arts/Shutterstock.com.

Library of Congress Cataloging-in-Publication Data

Lynette, Rachel.
 Rats / by Rachel Lynette. — 1st ed.
     p. cm. — (Monsters of the animal kingdom)
 Includes index.
 ISBN 978-1-4488-9630-1 (library binding) — ISBN 978-1-4488-9717-9 (pbk.) —
ISBN 978-1-4488-9718-6 (6-pack)
 1. Rats—Juvenile literature. I. Title.
 QL737.R666L96 2013
 599.35—dc23
                                2012016786

Manufactured in the United States of America

CPSIA Compliance Information: Batch #W13PK5: For Further Information contact Rosen Publishing, New York, New York at 1-800-237-9932

CONTENTS

WHAT ARE RATS?

Have you ever seen a rat? Maybe you have seen one scurrying across the road or being chased by a cat. Rats are a type of **rodent**. Mice, hamsters, moles, lemmings, and porcupines are also rodents. Like humans, rodents are **mammals**.

The brown rat, shown here, is also called the Norway rat. It was once thought that the rat first came from that country, but today scientists think it first came from central Asia.

The black rat, shown here, tends to have bigger ears and a pointier nose than the brown rat.

Some animals that have the word "rat" in their names are not really rats. These include pack rats and kangaroo rats. There are about 80 different **species** of true rats. This book will focus on the black rat and the brown rat because they are the most common of the true rats.

RAT PLANET!

Rats can be found on every continent except Antarctica. They can live in almost any kind of **climate** and habitat as long as they can find food, water, and shelter.

Some rats live in natural places, such as deserts, forests, or meadows. Groups of rats dig large burrows with many connecting tunnels, rooms, and entrances.

Rats do not mind getting wet. In fact, they often live near riverbanks because they can easily find food and water and make burrows there.

In cities, rats are often seen in parks, alleys, subway tunnels, and damp basements.

Many rats live near people. They are attracted to where people live because it is easy for them to find food and shelter. Rats can be found in barns, basements, garbage dumps, sewers, warehouses, and shipping docks.

BUILT TO SURVIVE

A rat's body looks a lot like a mouse's, but these animals are not the same! Rats are larger and have longer tails.

Rats have a strong sense of smell. They use their sense of smell to find food and to identify other rats. Rats also have excellent hearing, which helps them stay away from danger. Rats have poor eyesight, but their whiskers help them feel their way in the dark.

Rats have thick fur that keeps them dry and warm. Rats also have large, strong hind legs for running and climbing.

The brown rat's fur can be a mix of light brown, dark brown, and gray hairs.

POWERFUL TEETH

Rats have two types of teeth. Their four front teeth are called **incisors**. They are long, slightly curved and very strong. These four teeth never stop growing! As all rodents do, rats spend a lot of time **gnawing**. Gnawing grinds the incisors down and keeps them from

Here you can see a rat's incisors. The rat must gnaw on things to keep these teeth from becoming overgrown.

Left: The rat's strong, flexible paws are suited to digging burrows and picking through garbage for food. *Below*: Rats can gnaw through metal pipes in homes. They are also a common sight in city sewers, like the one shown here.

growing too long. Rats also have 12 molars at the backs of their mouths that are used for grinding their food.

A gnawing rat can mean trouble for people. Rats often damage buildings by gnawing holes in walls, floors, and doors. They also gnaw through electrical wires, cables, and even pipes!

SCARY FACTS

1 Rats have such strong teeth and jaws that they can chew through concrete!

2 If a rat stops gnawing, its front teeth will grow into long curves, making it difficult for the rat to eat.

3 Rats are good swimmers. They can swim up to .5 mile (805 m). They can tread water for three days!

12

4 When food is scarce, older members of a rat pack will try to attack and eat babies. Mother rats fight to protect their babies from being eaten.

5 In the **Middle Ages**, black rats spread black death, also called the plague, a deadly disease that killed one out of every three people in Europe.

6 The story of the Pied Piper is of a man who used music to first lure away all of a town's rats and then to lure away all the children!

7 Rats have been featured in several animated movies for kids including *Charlotte's Web* and *Ratatouille*.

8 Ron Weasley's pet rat Scabbers played a significant role in the Harry Potter books and movies.

9 A German legend states that a group of rats can get their tails tangled and form a giant ball called a Rat King.

DINNERTIME!

Rats will eat almost anything! Rats living in the wild will eat berries, seeds, insects, and worms. They will also catch small fish in rivers and ponds. They will even eat the remains of animals that are already dead. Rats that live on farms will eat grains from fields and storehouses.

This rat is having a bit of pie that was left out. Rats are not picky eaters, though!

These rats have broken into sacks of grain. Grains of any kind are one of the rat's preferred foods.

Rats in cities survive mostly on food that humans throw away and will eat whatever they find. Rats have excellent memories. When a rat finds a good source of food, it will return to it again and again.

RT OF THE PACK

...ve in groups, called packs or colonies. The rats ...colony mark their **territory** with urine. Other ...ell the urine and know to keep away. Sometimes ...om different colonies fight over the territory.

...ir of adult
...with a pair
...ts.

Male rats will fight over territory or over females. A rat that is ready to fight comes up on its back legs to challenge the other rats.

Rats in the same colony usually get along well together. If a new male rat wants to join a colony, it will have to fight the male rats that are already part of it. If the newcomer wins, it joins the colony. If it loses, it looks for another colony to join.

BABY RATS

After **mating**, a female rat will give birth to 6 to 12 babies after about 23 days. Newborn rats are blind, deaf, hairless, and helpless. The mother cares for her babies and **nurses** them several times a day. Male rats do not take care of the babies at all.

The mother rat tends to her young until they are weaned. Mothers often spend more time caring for smaller litters because more of these babies are likely to survive.

A female rat can have up to five litters each year!

Baby rats grow hair by one week of age. By the time they are two weeks old, they can see and hear and start to leave the nest with their mother. Young rats are **weaned** at three weeks.

RAT PREDATORS

Rats make a tasty meal for many **predators**, including owls, hawks, snakes, raccoons, and weasels. Cats and dogs also **prey** on rats. In some countries, such as Cambodia, China, India, and Zimbabwe, people sometimes hunt and eat rats.

This African wild dog has caught a rat and is eating it.

Owls, such as this spotted eagle owl, hunt at night when rats are more active. They are a major rat predator.

To protect themselves from predators, rats try to avoid open areas where they could be easily attacked. Rats can live up to three years, but most do not survive to their first birthday. Rat predators play an important role. Without so many predators,

PEST OR PET?

Most people do not like rats. Rats cause billions of dollars in food and property loss every year. They also spread several life-threatening sicknesses. For these reasons, rats are considered pests and are often killed by humans.

However, some types of rats help people. Scientists use special lab rats to make sure that new medicines are safe. **Domesticated** rats are often sold as pets.

Lab rats, like the one shown here, are used in medical research. Rats are used in labs because they reproduce often, and they are easy to care for.

GLOSSARY

climate (KLY-mut) The kind of weather a certain place has.

domesticated (duh-MES-tih-kayt-ed) Raised to live with people.

gnawing (NAW-ing) Keeping on biting something.

incisors (in-SY-zurz) An animal's four front teeth used for cutting.

mammals (MA-mulz) Warm-blooded animals that have backbones and hair, breathe air, and feed milk to their young.

mating (MAYT-ing) Coming together to make babies.

Middle Ages (MIH-dul AY-jez) The period in European history from about AD 500 to about 1450.

nurses (NURS-ez) When a female feeds her baby milk from her body.

predators (PREH-duh-terz) Animals that kill other animals for food.

prey (PRAY) To hunt for food.

rodent (ROH-dent) An animal with gnawing teeth, such as a mouse.

species (SPEE-sheez) One kind of living thing. All people are one species.

territory (TER-uh-tor-ee) Land or space that animals guard for their use.

weaned (WEEND) Changed a baby's food from a mother's milk to solid food.

INDEX

WEBSITES

Due to the changing nature of Internet links, PowerKids Press has developed an online list of websites related to the subject of this book. This site is updated regularly. Please use this link to access the list: www.powerkidslinks.com/mak/rats/